God Made Easter

Catholic Easter Book for Children

Printed in the USA

God made Easter, a gift for you

For God so loved the world that he gave his
one and only Son

-John 3:16

Tulips open, new buds bloom

He has given us new birth

1 Peter 1:3

Look what Spring will bring

Easter time is here again

Jesus said, "I am the resurrection and the life." – John 11:25

Church bells ring

Jesus our Savior has risen!

He is not here, he is risen

– Matt. 28:6

Great joy fills our heart

I will sing for joy
-Psalm 63:7

Baby bunnies, baby chicks, baby birds, eggs in a nest

All things are new, all things are bright

Now all things are new

– 2 Corinthians 5:17

God sent us His only Son, Jesus, the gift of everlasting life

We celebrate, dance and sing.

God made Easter, the most precious thing.

Green grass, little bugs, joyful laughter, great big hugs

We are alive in God, through Jesus Christ

– Romans 6:11

God made Easter to show you His love

Our hearts are happy, our
Easter baskets are full

God blesses you...
– Psalm 2:12

Everlasting life is God's Easter gift to you

If you believe, you will have everlasting life

– John 11:25

The Sign of the Cross

In the name of the Father, and of the Son, and of the Holy Spirit, Amen.

Hail Mary

Hail Mary full of Grace, the Lord is with thee. Blessed are thou among women and blessed is the fruit of thy womb Jesus. Holy Mary Mother of God, pray for us sinners now and at the hour of our death Amen.

Jesus, Mary and Joseph, Pray for Us

Our Father

Our Father, Who art in Heaven, hallowed be Thy name; Thy Kingdom come, Thy will be done on earth as it is in Heaven. Give us this day our daily bread; and forgive us our trespasses as we forgive those who trespass against us; and lead us not into temptation, but deliver us from evil. Amen.

Glory Be

Glory be to the Father and to the Son and to the Holy Spirit. As it was in the beginning is now, and ever shall be, world without end. Amen.

Made in the USA
Monee, IL
11 March 2021